Travel Journal

If found, please return to

_____

_____

about me

Name

_____

Date of birth   Nationality

_____   _____

Country of residence

_____

My first trip away was to

_____

_____

My favorite memory from past travels is

_____

_____

_____

_____

I love to travel because

_____

_____

My number one city to visit is

_____

_____

My favorite country to travel to is

_____

_____

My preferred kind of trip is

_____

_____

_____

If I could be anywhere, I'd choose

_____

_____

_____

I bought/received this travel journal because

_____

_____

_____

_____

My bucket list

Places I want to visit

Food and drink I want to try

Sights I want to see

○
○
○
○
○
○
○
○
○
○
○
○

○
○
○
○
○
○
○
○
○
○
○
○

Experiences I want to have

○
○
○
○
○
○
○
○
○
○
○
○

Handy translations

English	French	Spanish	Portuguese
Hello	Bonjour	Hola	Olá
How are you?	Ça va?	¿Cómo estás?	Como está?
Goodbye	Au revoir	Adiós	Adeus
Thank you	Merci	Gracias	Obrigado
Excuse me	Excusez-moi	Disculpe	Com licença
The bill, please	L'addition, s'il vous plaît	La cuenta, por favor	A conta, por favor
How much is this?	C'est combien?	¿Cuánto cuesta?	Quanto custa isso?
Can you help me?	Pouvez-vous m'aider?	¿Puede ayudarme?	Pode me ajudar
Do you speak English?	Vous parlez anglais?	¿Habla usted inglés?	Você fala inglês?

Hindi	German	Japanese	Mandarin
Namaskār/Namasté	Hallo	Konnichiwa	Nǐ hǎo
Āp kaise haim?	Wie geht es Ihnen?	O-genki desuka?	Nǐ hǎoma?
Namaskār/Namasté	Auf Wiedersehen	Sayohnara	Zàijiàn
Dhanyavād	Danke	Arigatō	(fēicháng) xièxienǐ
Māf kījiegā	Entschuldigung	Sumimasen	Láojià
Kyā hamem bil mil saktā hai	Die Rechnung, bitte	Kaikei o onegaishimasu	Qǐng gěiwo zhàngdān
Iska kya dam hai?	Wie viel kostet das?	Kore wa ikura desuka?	Zhège duōshǎoqián?
Kyā āp merī sahāyatā kar sakte/saktī haim?	Können sie mir helfen?	Tasukete kudasai?	Nǐ néng bāngbang wǒ ma?
Kyā āp an grezī bolte haim?	Sprechen sie Englisch?	Eigo o hanasemasuka?	nǐ huì shuō yīngwén ma?

Other useful phrases

Useful conversions

SPEED

mph	20	30	40	50	60	70	80	90	100
km/h	32	48	64	80	96	112	128	144	160

LENGTHS	DISTANCES
1cm	0.39 in
1m	3.28 ft
1m	1.09 yd
1km	0.62 mi
1in	2.54 cm
1ft	30.48 cm
1yd	0.91 m
1mi	1.6 km

MEASURES	WEIGHTS
½oz / 1 tbsp	15g
1oz / 2 tbsp	29g
5oz	141g
8oz / 1 cup	226g
10oz	283g
15oz / 2 cups	425g
1lb	453g

TEMPERATURE

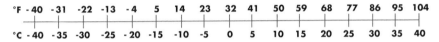

°F	- 40	-31	-22	-13	- 4	5	14	23	32	41	50	59	68	77	86	95	104
°C	- 40	-35	-30	-25	- 20	-15	-10	-5	0	5	10	15	20	25	30	35	40

Other useful information

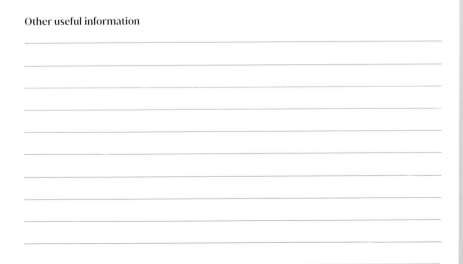

World map

ARCTIC
OCEAN

GREENLAND

Arctic Circle

ALASKA
(USA)
–9

–7

CANADA

ICELAND
+0

UNITED
KINGDOM
+0

IRELAND

FRA

–5

–4

–3½

PACIFIC
OCEAN

–7

–6

–5

UNITED STATES
OF AMERICA

NORTH
ATLANTIC
OCEAN

SPAIN
+1

PORTUGAL
+0

MOROCCO
+1

ALG

–10

HAWAII
(USA)

MEXICO

HONDURAS

THE
BAHAMAS

CUBA

DOMINICAN
REPUBLIC

MAURITANIA
+0

SENEGAL

+0

–6

JAMAICA

PUERTO
RICO

BARBADOS

MALI

GUATEMALA

–5

TRINIDAD & TOBAGO

GUINEA

–6

COSTA RICA
PANAMA

VENEZUELA

COLOMBIA

GUYANA
SURINAME
FRENCH GUIANA

GHAN

Equator

ECUADOR

PERU

BRAZIL

–10

FRENCH
POLYNESIA

PACIFIC
OCEAN

BOLIVIA

PARAGUAY

SOUTH
ATLANTIC
OCEAN

CHILE
–4

–3

URUGUAY

ARGENTINA

SOUTHERN OCEAN

Antarctic Circle

| -11 | -10 | -9 | -8 | -7 | -6 | -5 | -4 | -3 | -2 | -1 | 0 |

Green
Meri

Hours Behind Greenwich Mean Time

ARCTIC OCEAN

Arctic Circle

RUSSIA

+12 −12

+10

+11   +12

+2
|LAND
|ONIA   +3   +5   +7   +9
|TVIA
|NIA   +4
|ELARUS
|KRAINE   +4   +6   −10
| +2   +5
|ANIA   KAZAKHSTAN
|GARIA   UZBEKISTAN
| +3   +4   TURKMENISTAN KYRGYZSTAN   MONGOLIA
TURKEY   TAJIKISTAN   +8   N.KOREA   JAPAN
                                                                                          +9
CYPRUS   IRAQ   IRAN   AFGHANISTAN   CHINA   SOUTH
                       +3½   +4½   +8   KOREA
EGYPT   PAKISTAN NEPAL BHUTAN
       SAUDI   U.A.E.   +5¾   LAOS   +9   +10   +11   +12
       ARABIA   International Date Line
   +2   +3   OMAN   INDIA   MYAN-   +8
|SUDAN   YEMEN   +5½   BANGLA- MAR
                                      DESH   +6½
                       SOMALIA   THAILAND VIETNAM   MARSHALL
SOUTH ETHIOPIA   CAMBODIA   ISLANDS
SUDAN   +3   SRI   PHILIPPINES   +12
UGANDA   MALDIVES   LANKA   Equator
|OF   KENYA   +5   MALAYSIA   PALAU
TANZANIA   PAPUA
                                      SINGAPORE   INDONESIA +9 NEW
|ABIA MOZAMBIQUE   INDIAN   GUINEA   SOLOMON
                      OCEAN   +10   ISLANDS
|ZIMBA-
|BWE   MADAGASCAR   +11
|NA   +3   MAURITIUS   AUSTRALIA   VANUATU   FIJI
|TH   +4   +12
|CA   +8   +8½   +10   NEW
                                                                                     CALEDONIA

                                                                                               NEW
                                                                                               ZEALAND
                                                                                               +12

SOUTHERN OCEAN

Antarctic Circle

| +2 | +3 | +4 | +5 | +6 | +7 | +8 | +9 | +10 | +11 | International Date Line |

Hours Ahead of Greenwich Mean Time

Journey 1

Where I'm going

_____

Where I'm staying

_____

_____

Mark where you're going

Reasons for going

_____

_____

_____

_____

Dates   Who with

_____   _____

_____   _____

_____   _____

The plan

_____

_____

_____

_____

My hopes and wishes for the trip

I'm most excited about

_____

_____

The first place I want to visit is

_____

_____

Of course I'll be trying

_____

_____

I'm hoping for

_____

_____

Journey planner

Monday	Tuesday	Wednesday	Thursda

Friday	Saturday	Sunday

Accommodations details

Notes

"I never travel without my diary. One
should always have something sensational
to read in the train."

Oscar Wilde, *The Importance of Being Earnest*

Packing list

Category _____

- ○ _____
- ○ _____
- ○ _____
- ○ _____
- ○ _____
- ○ _____
- ○ _____
- ○ _____
- ○ _____
- ○ _____
- ○ _____
- ○ _____

Category _____

- ○ _____
- ○ _____
- ○ _____
- ○ _____
- ○ _____
- ○ _____
- ○ _____
- ○ _____
- ○ _____
- ○ _____
- ○ _____
- ○ _____

Category _____

- ○ _____
- ○ _____
- ○ _____
- ○ _____
- ○ _____
- ○ _____
- ○ _____
- ○ _____
- ○ _____
- ○ _____
- ○ _____
- ○ _____

Category _____

- ○ _____
- ○ _____
- ○ _____
- ○ _____
- ○ _____
- ○ _____
- ○ _____
- ○ _____
- ○ _____
- ○ _____
- ○ _____
- ○ _____

Budget

Item or experience	Budgeted	Spent

Total budgeted

Total spent

What was your most memorable meal?

What happened on your favorite day?

What was your favorite evening?

Best conversation you had?

What would you do again?

What will you recommend to others?

What I've learned about me

Message to myself

My reviews

What

My review

/10

What

My review

/10

What

My review

/10

What

My review

/10

What

My review

/10

What

My review

/10

What

My review

/10

What

My review

/10

Journey 2

Where I'm going

_____

Where I'm staying

_____

_____

Mark where you're going

Reasons for going

_____
_____
_____
_____

Dates   Who with

_____   _____
_____   _____
_____   _____

The plan

_____
_____
_____
_____

My hopes and wishes for the trip

I'm most excited about

_____
_____

The first place I want to visit is

_____
_____

Of course I'll be trying

_____
_____

I'm hoping for

_____
_____

Journey planner

Monday	Tuesday	Wednesday	Thursda

Friday	Saturday	Sunday

Accommodations details

_____
_____
_____
_____
_____
_____
_____
_____
_____
_____

Notes

_____
_____
_____
_____
_____
_____
_____
_____
_____
_____
_____

"I never travel without my diary. One
should always have something sensational
to read in the train."

Oscar Wilde, _The Importance of Being Earnest_

Packing list

Category_____

- ○ _____
- ○ _____
- ○ _____
- ○ _____
- ○ _____
- ○ _____
- ○ _____
- ○ _____
- ○ _____
- ○ _____
- ○ _____
- ○ _____

Category_____

- ○ _____
- ○ _____
- ○ _____
- ○ _____
- ○ _____
- ○ _____
- ○ _____
- ○ _____
- ○ _____
- ○ _____
- ○ _____
- ○ _____

Category_____

- ○ _____
- ○ _____
- ○ _____
- ○ _____
- ○ _____
- ○ _____
- ○ _____
- ○ _____
- ○ _____
- ○ _____
- ○ _____
- ○ _____

Category_____

- ○ _____
- ○ _____
- ○ _____
- ○ _____
- ○ _____
- ○ _____
- ○ _____
- ○ _____
- ○ _____
- ○ _____
- ○ _____
- ○ _____

Budget

Item or experience	Budgeted	Spent

Total budgeted   Total spent

6

What was your most memorable meal?

What happened on your favorite day?

What was your favorite evening?

Best conversation you had?

What would you do again?

What will you recommend to others?

What I've learned about me

Message to myself

My reviews

What

_____

_____

_____

My review

_____

_____

_____

_____

_____

/10

What

_____

_____

_____

My review

_____

_____

_____

_____

_____

/10

What

_____

_____

_____

My review

_____

_____

_____

_____

_____

/10

What

_____

_____

_____

My review

_____

_____

_____

_____

_____

/10

What

My review

/10

What

My review

/10

What

My review

/10

What

My review

/10

Journey 3

Where I'm going

_____

Where I'm staying

_____

_____

Mark where you're going

Reasons for going

_____

_____

_____

_____

Dates

_____

_____

_____

Who with

_____

_____

_____

The plan

_____

_____

_____

_____

My hopes and wishes for the trip

I'm most excited about

_____

_____

The first place I want to visit is

_____

_____

Of course I'll be trying

_____

_____

I'm hoping for

_____

_____

Journey planner

Monday	Tuesday	Wednesday	Thursday

Friday	Saturday	Sunday

Accommodations details

_____
_____
_____
_____
_____
_____
_____
_____
_____
_____
_____
_____

Notes

_____
_____
_____
_____
_____
_____
_____
_____
_____
_____
_____
_____

"I never travel without my diary. One
should always have something sensational
to read in the train."

Oscar Wilde, _The Importance of Being Earnest_

Packing list

Category_____

- ○ _____
- ○ _____
- ○ _____
- ○ _____
- ○ _____
- ○ _____
- ○ _____
- ○ _____
- ○ _____
- ○ _____
- ○ _____
- ○ _____

Category_____

- ○ _____
- ○ _____
- ○ _____
- ○ _____
- ○ _____
- ○ _____
- ○ _____
- ○ _____
- ○ _____
- ○ _____
- ○ _____
- ○ _____

Category_____

- ○ _____
- ○ _____
- ○ _____
- ○ _____
- ○ _____
- ○ _____
- ○ _____
- ○ _____
- ○ _____
- ○ _____
- ○ _____
- ○ _____

Category_____

- ○ _____
- ○ _____
- ○ _____
- ○ _____
- ○ _____
- ○ _____
- ○ _____
- ○ _____
- ○ _____
- ○ _____
- ○ _____
- ○ _____

Budget

Item or experience	Budgeted	Spent

Total budgeted

Total spent

What was your most memorable meal?

What happened on your favorite day?

What was your favorite evening?

Best conversation you had?

What would you do again?

What will you recommend to others?

What I've learned about me

Message to myself

My reviews

What

My review

/10

What

My review

/10

What

My review

/10

What

My review

/10

What

My review

/10

What

My review

/10

What

My review

/10

What

My review

/10

Journey 4

Where I'm going

_____

Where I'm staying

_____

_____

Mark where you're going

Reasons for going

_____

_____

_____

_____

Dates   Who with

_____   _____

_____   _____

_____   _____

The plan

_____

_____

_____

_____

My hopes and wishes for the trip

I'm most excited about

_____

_____

The first place I want to visit is

_____

_____

Of course I'll be trying

_____

_____

I'm hoping for

_____

_____

Journey planner

Monday	Tuesday	Wednesday	Thursday

Friday	Saturday	Sunday

Accommodations details

_____
_____
_____
_____
_____
_____
_____
_____
_____
_____

Notes

_____
_____
_____
_____
_____
_____
_____
_____
_____
_____

"I never travel without my diary. One
should always have something sensational
to read in the train."

Oscar Wilde, *The Importance of Being Earnest*

Packing list

Category_____

Category_____

Category_____

Category_____

Budget

Item or experience	Budgeted	Spent

Total budgeted

Total spent

What was your most memorable meal?

What happened on your favorite day?

What was your favorite evening?

What would you do again?

What will you recommend to others?

What I've learned about me

Message to myself

My reviews

What

_____

_____

_____

My review

_____

_____

_____

_____

/10

What

_____

_____

_____

My review

_____

_____

_____

_____

/10

What

_____

_____

_____

My review

_____

_____

_____

_____

/10

What

_____

_____

_____

My review

_____

_____

_____

_____

/10

What

My review

/10

What

My review

/10

What

My review

/10

What

My review

/10

Journey 5

Where I'm going

_____

Where I'm staying

_____

_____

Mark where you're going

Reasons for going

_____
_____
_____
_____

Dates   Who with

_____   _____
_____   _____
_____   _____

The plan

_____
_____
_____
_____

My hopes and wishes for the trip

I'm most excited about

_____
_____

The first place I want to visit is

_____
_____

Of course I'll be trying

_____
_____

I'm hoping for

_____
_____

Journey planner

Monday	Tuesday	Wednesday	Thursday

Friday	Saturday	Sunday

Accommodations details

_____
_____
_____
_____
_____
_____
_____
_____
_____
_____

Notes

_____
_____
_____
_____
_____
_____
_____
_____
_____
_____
_____

"I never travel without my diary. One should always have something sensational to read in the train."

Oscar Wilde, _The Importance of Being Earnest_

Packing list

Category _____

- ○ _____
- ○ _____
- ○ _____
- ○ _____
- ○ _____
- ○ _____
- ○ _____
- ○ _____
- ○ _____
- ○ _____
- ○ _____
- ○ _____

Category _____

- ○ _____
- ○ _____
- ○ _____
- ○ _____
- ○ _____
- ○ _____
- ○ _____
- ○ _____
- ○ _____
- ○ _____
- ○ _____
- ○ _____

Category _____

- ○ _____
- ○ _____
- ○ _____
- ○ _____
- ○ _____
- ○ _____
- ○ _____
- ○ _____
- ○ _____
- ○ _____
- ○ _____
- ○ _____

Category _____

- ○ _____
- ○ _____
- ○ _____
- ○ _____
- ○ _____
- ○ _____
- ○ _____
- ○ _____
- ○ _____
- ○ _____
- ○ _____
- ○ _____

Budget

Item or experience	Budgeted	Spent

Total budgeted   Total spent

What was your most memorable meal?

What happened on your favorite day?

What was your favorite evening?

Best conversation you had?

What would you do again?

What I've learned about me

Message to myself

My reviews

What

My review

/10

What

My review

/10

What

My review

/10

What

My review

/10

What

My review

/10

What

My review

/10

What

My review

/10

What

My review

/10

Journey 6

Where I'm going

_____

Where I'm staying

_____

_____

Mark where you're going

Reasons for going

_____

_____

_____

_____

Dates   Who with

_____   _____

_____   _____

_____   _____

The plan

_____

_____

_____

_____

My hopes and wishes for the trip

I'm most excited about

_____

_____

The first place I want to visit is

_____

_____

Of course I'll be trying

_____

_____

I'm hoping for

_____

_____

Journey planner

Monday	Tuesday	Wednesday	Thursda

Friday	Saturday	Sunday

Accommodations details

_____
_____
_____
_____
_____
_____
_____
_____
_____
_____

Notes

_____
_____
_____
_____
_____
_____
_____
_____
_____
_____

"I never travel without my diary. One should always have something sensational to read in the train."

Oscar Wilde, *The Importance of Being Earnest*

Packing list

Category_____

- ○ _____
- ○ _____
- ○ _____
- ○ _____
- ○ _____
- ○ _____
- ○ _____
- ○ _____
- ○ _____
- ○ _____
- ○ _____
- ○ _____

Category_____

- ○ _____
- ○ _____
- ○ _____
- ○ _____
- ○ _____
- ○ _____
- ○ _____
- ○ _____
- ○ _____
- ○ _____
- ○ _____
- ○ _____

Category_____

- ○ _____
- ○ _____
- ○ _____
- ○ _____
- ○ _____
- ○ _____
- ○ _____
- ○ _____
- ○ _____
- ○ _____
- ○ _____
- ○ _____

Category_____

- ○ _____
- ○ _____
- ○ _____
- ○ _____
- ○ _____
- ○ _____
- ○ _____
- ○ _____
- ○ _____
- ○ _____
- ○ _____
- ○ _____

Budget

Item or experience	Budgeted	Spent

Total budgeted

Total spent

What was your most memorable meal?

What happened on your favorite day?

What was your favorite evening?

Best conversation you had?

What would you do again?

What will you recommend to others?

What I've learned about me

Message to myself

My reviews

What
_____
_____
_____

My review
_____
_____
_____
_____
_____

/10

What
_____
_____
_____

My review
_____
_____
_____
_____
_____

/10

What
_____
_____
_____

My review
_____
_____
_____
_____
_____

/10

What
_____
_____
_____

My review
_____
_____
_____
_____
_____

/10

What

My review

/10

What

My review

/10

What

My review

/10

What

My review

/10

Journey 7

Where I'm going

_____

Where I'm staying

_____

_____

Mark where you're going

Reasons for going

Dates

Who with

The plan

My hopes and wishes for the trip

I'm most excited about

The first place I want to visit is

Of course I'll be trying

I'm hoping for

Journey planner

Monday	Tuesday	Wednesday	Thursday

Friday	Saturday	Sunday

Accommodations details

_____
_____
_____
_____
_____
_____
_____
_____
_____
_____

Notes

_____
_____
_____
_____
_____
_____
_____
_____
_____
_____
_____

"I never travel without my diary. One
   should always have something sensational
   to read in the train."

Oscar Wilde, *The Importance of Being Earnest*

Packing list

Category_____

- ○ _____
- ○ _____
- ○ _____
- ○ _____
- ○ _____
- ○ _____
- ○ _____
- ○ _____
- ○ _____
- ○ _____
- ○ _____

Category_____

- ○ _____
- ○ _____
- ○ _____
- ○ _____
- ○ _____
- ○ _____
- ○ _____
- ○ _____
- ○ _____
- ○ _____
- ○ _____

Category_____

- ○ _____
- ○ _____
- ○ _____
- ○ _____
- ○ _____
- ○ _____
- ○ _____
- ○ _____
- ○ _____
- ○ _____
- ○ _____

Category_____

- ○ _____
- ○ _____
- ○ _____
- ○ _____
- ○ _____
- ○ _____
- ○ _____
- ○ _____
- ○ _____
- ○ _____
- ○ _____

Budget

Item or experience	Budgeted	Spent

Total budgeted   Total spent

What was your most memorable meal?

What happened on your favorite day?

What was your favorite evening?

Best conversation you had?

What would you do again?

What will you recommend to others?

What I've learned about me

Message to myself

My reviews

What
_____
_____
_____

My review
_____
_____
_____
_____
_____

What
_____
_____
_____

My review
_____
_____
_____
_____
_____

What
_____
_____
_____

My review
_____
_____
_____
_____
_____

What
_____
_____
_____

My review
_____
_____
_____
_____
_____

What

My review

/10

What

My review

/10

What

My review

/10

What

My review

/10

Journey 8

Where I'm going

_____

Where I'm staying

_____
_____

Mark where you're going

Reasons for going

_____
_____
_____
_____

Dates   Who with

_____   _____
_____   _____
_____   _____

The plan

_____
_____
_____
_____

My hopes and wishes for the trip

I'm most excited about

_____
_____

The first place I want to visit is

_____
_____

Of course I'll be trying

_____
_____

I'm hoping for

_____
_____

Journey planner

Monday	Tuesday	Wednesday	Thursday

Friday	Saturday	Sunday

Accommodations details

_____

_____

_____

_____

_____

_____

_____

_____

_____

_____

Notes

_____

_____

_____

_____

_____

_____

_____

_____

_____

_____

"I never travel without my diary. One
should always have something sensational
to read in the train."

Oscar Wilde, *The Importance of Being Earnest*

Packing list

Category _____

- ○ _____
- ○ _____
- ○ _____
- ○ _____
- ○ _____
- ○ _____
- ○ _____
- ○ _____
- ○ _____
- ○ _____
- ○ _____
- ○ _____

Category _____

- ○ _____
- ○ _____
- ○ _____
- ○ _____
- ○ _____
- ○ _____
- ○ _____
- ○ _____
- ○ _____
- ○ _____
- ○ _____
- ○ _____

Category _____

- ○ _____
- ○ _____
- ○ _____
- ○ _____
- ○ _____
- ○ _____
- ○ _____
- ○ _____
- ○ _____
- ○ _____
- ○ _____
- ○ _____

Category _____

- ○ _____
- ○ _____
- ○ _____
- ○ _____
- ○ _____
- ○ _____
- ○ _____
- ○ _____
- ○ _____
- ○ _____
- ○ _____
- ○ _____

Budget

Item or experience	Budgeted	Spent

Total budgeted

Total spent

What was your most memorable meal?

What happened on your favorite day?

What was your favorite evening?

Best conversation you had?

What would you do again?

What will you recommend to others?

What I've learned about me

Message to myself

My reviews

What

_____

_____

_____

My review

_____

_____

_____

_____

_____

/10

What

_____

_____

_____

My review

_____

_____

_____

_____

_____

/10

What

_____

_____

_____

My review

_____

_____

_____

_____

_____

/10

What

_____

_____

_____

My review

_____

_____

_____

_____

_____

/10

What

_____

_____

_____

My review

_____

_____

_____

_____

_____

/10

What

_____

_____

_____

My review

_____

_____

_____

_____

_____

/10

What

_____

_____

_____

My review

_____

_____

_____

_____

_____

/10

What

_____

_____

_____

My review

_____

_____

_____

_____

_____

/10

Journey 9

Where I'm going

_____

Where I'm staying

_____

_____

Mark where you're going

Reasons for going

_____
_____
_____
_____

Dates   Who with

_____   _____
_____   _____
_____   _____

The plan

_____
_____
_____
_____

My hopes and wishes for the trip

I'm most excited about

_____
_____

The first place I want to visit is

_____
_____

Of course I'll be trying

_____
_____

I'm hoping for

_____
_____

Journey planner

Monday	Tuesday	Wednesday	Thursday

Friday	Saturday	Sunday

Accommodations details

_____
_____
_____
_____
_____
_____
_____
_____
_____
_____

Notes

_____
_____
_____
_____
_____
_____
_____
_____
_____
_____

"I never travel without my diary. One
should always have something sensational
to read in the train."

Oscar Wilde, *The Importance of Being Earnest*

Packing list

Category_____

- ○ _____
- ○ _____
- ○ _____
- ○ _____
- ○ _____
- ○ _____
- ○ _____
- ○ _____
- ○ _____
- ○ _____
- ○ _____

Category_____

- ○ _____
- ○ _____
- ○ _____
- ○ _____
- ○ _____
- ○ _____
- ○ _____
- ○ _____
- ○ _____
- ○ _____
- ○ _____

Category_____

- ○ _____
- ○ _____
- ○ _____
- ○ _____
- ○ _____
- ○ _____
- ○ _____
- ○ _____
- ○ _____
- ○ _____
- ○ _____
- ○ _____

Category_____

- ○ _____
- ○ _____
- ○ _____
- ○ _____
- ○ _____
- ○ _____
- ○ _____
- ○ _____
- ○ _____
- ○ _____
- ○ _____
- ○ _____

Budget

Item or experience	Budgeted	Spent

Total budgeted

Total spent

What was your most memorable meal?

What happened on your favorite day?

What was your favorite evening?

Best conversation you had?

What would you do again?

What will you recommend to others?

What I've learned about me

Message to myself

My reviews

What

My review

/10

What

My review

/10

What

My review

/10

What

My review

/10

What

My review

/10

What

My review

/10

What

My review

/10

What

My review

/10

Journey 10

Where I'm going

_____

Where I'm staying

_____

_____

Mark where you're going

Reasons for going

_____

_____

_____

_____

Dates   Who with

_____   _____

_____   _____

_____   _____

The plan

_____

_____

_____

_____

My hopes and wishes for the trip

I'm most excited about

_____

_____

The first place I want to visit is

_____

_____

Of course I'll be trying

_____

_____

I'm hoping for

_____

_____

Journey planner

Monday	Tuesday	Wednesday	Thursday

Friday	Saturday	Sunday

Accommodations details

Notes

"I never travel without my diary. One should always have something sensational to read in the train."

Oscar Wilde, *The Importance of Being Earnest*

Packing list

Category_____ _____

- ○ _____
- ○ _____
- ○ _____
- ○ _____
- ○ _____
- ○ _____
- ○ _____
- ○ _____
- ○ _____
- ○ _____
- ○ _____
- ○ _____

Category_____

- ○ _____
- ○ _____
- ○ _____
- ○ _____
- ○ _____
- ○ _____
- ○ _____
- ○ _____
- ○ _____
- ○ _____
- ○ _____
- ○ _____

Category_____

- ○ _____
- ○ _____
- ○ _____
- ○ _____
- ○ _____
- ○ _____
- ○ _____
- ○ _____
- ○ _____
- ○ _____
- ○ _____
- ○ _____

Category_____

- ○ _____
- ○ _____
- ○ _____
- ○ _____
- ○ _____
- ○ _____
- ○ _____
- ○ _____
- ○ _____
- ○ _____
- ○ _____
- ○ _____

Budget

Item or experience	Budgeted	Spent

Total budgeted

Total spent

What was your most memorable meal?

What happened on your favorite day?

What was your favorite evening?

Best conversation you had?

What would you do again?

What will you recommend to others?

What I've learned about me

Message to myself

My reviews

What

My review

/10

What

My review

/10

What

My review

/10

What

My review

/10

What

My review

/10

What

My review

/10

What

My review

/10

What

My review

/10

Notes

Jacket Illustrator Marina Ester Castaldo

Published in Great Britain by Dorling Kindersley Limited, DK, One Embassy Gardens, 8 Viaduct Gardens, London SW11 7BW
The authorised representative in the EEA is Dorling Kindersley Verlag GmbH. Arnulfstr.124, 80636 Munich, Germany

ISBN: 978 0 2416 2726 6

Printed and bound in Malaysia.

www.dk.com

This book was made with Forest
Stewardship Council™ certified
paper – one small step in DK's
commitment to a sustainable future.
Learn more at
www.dk.com/uk/information/sustainability